FAIRACRES PUBLI

# LOVING
## YOURSELF

RICHARD FROST

© 2025 SLG Press
First Edition 2025

FAIRACRES PUBLICATIONS 230

ISBN 978-0-7283-0423-9
Fairacres Publications Series ISSN 0307-1405

Richard Frost asserts the right to be identified as the author of this work, in accordance with the Copyright Designs and Patents act, 1988.

All rights reserved. No part of this publication may be reproduced, stored in a retrieval system, or transmitted, in any form or by any means, electronic, mechanical, photocopying, recording or otherwise, without the prior permission of the copyright owner.
No part of this book may be used or reproduced in any manner for the purpose of training artificial intelligence technologies or systems. In accordance with Article 4(3) of the DSM Directive 2019/790, SLG Press expressly reserves this work from the text and data mining exception.

The publishers have no control over, or responsibility for, any third-party website referred to in this book. All internet addresses given in this book were correct at the time of going to press. The authors and publisher regret any inconvenience caused if addresses have changed or sites have ceased to exist, but can accept no responsibility for any such changes.

Biblical quotations are taken from the New Revised Standard Version of the Bible unless otherwise noted.

Edited and typeset in Palatino Linotype by Julia Craig-McFeely

Front cover: 'Be Kind to Yourself' by Rachel Alice Leggett. First published in Lydia Rolley, *The Fatigue Book* (Hammersmith Books Limited, 2022). Used by kind permission.

SLG Press
Convent of the Incarnation
Fairacres • Oxford
www.slgpress.co.uk

Printed by
Grosvenor Group Ltd, Loughton, Essex

# CONTENTS

| | | |
|---|---|---|
| | Foreword *by Canon Deborah Parsons* | iii |
| | Acknowledgements | iv |
| | Introduction | 1 |
| 1 | The Second Commandment | 3 |
| 2 | What is Love? | 11 |
| 3 | Knowing God's Love | 18 |
| 4 | Intentional Attention | 23 |
| 5 | Day to Day | 26 |
| | Sources and Resources Mentioned in the Text | 37 |

# FOREWORD

In May 2023, I invited Richard Frost to speak at Holy Ground at Exeter Cathedral. His theme: Loving Yourself. In his reflections, he explored the well-known words, 'You shall love your neighbour as yourself.' He posited that most people feel comfortable with the concept of loving our neighbour but he asked, how do we love ourselves in the same way as we love others?

In this short book, Richard explores how love for ourselves originates from God's love for us and asks how we can love ourselves in a way that is neither self-absorbed nor narcissistic. He engages with both the head and the heart, wrestling with some of the issues and offering kernels of wisdom gleaned from his own experience and from other people, as well as signposting practical self-help.

The book touches on aspects of spirituality, identity and wellbeing and explores the human condition: what helps us to make choices between good, better or best, balancing love of neighbour with appropriate self-care and love of ourselves; how we can nurture purity of heart, secure in the knowledge that God's love for us is based not on anything we do or achieve, but on the premise that God is love; how we can allow the raw material of our lives to be transformed by the grace of God's unconditional love.

This is a book to linger with and to apply to daily living and spiritual practice. It is a book that is compassionate and realistic, honest and accessible, offering down-to-earth tips borne from lived experience and forged in the furnace of life. There is something in it for everyone. Drink deeply from this wisdom well and trust that the living water it contains will nourish the parched or dry places in yourself.

CANON DEBORAH PARSONS<br>CANON CHANCELLOR, EXETER CATHEDRAL

## ACKNOWLEDGEMENTS

This book developed following an invitation by Canon Deborah Parsons to give a talk on loving yourself at Exeter Cathedral in May 2023. I continue to be grateful to Deborah for her encouragement and fellowship both at the Cathedral and when she was Team Vicar on the Totnes Ministry Team in Devon, and for writing the Foreword to this book.

I am also immensely grateful to the people who provided personal contributions to me via email or in response to online posts seeking views and opinions. Those enabled such a publication as this to be grounded in the realities of day-to-day living and faith; I hope that you will be able to relate to their experiences as well.

My thanks also to Jane, Jon and Rachel for their encouragement, and others who have supported the writing journey, including my editor at SLG Press.

RICHARD FROST

# LOVING YOURSELF

# INTRODUCTION

'You shall love your neighbour as yourself' (Mark 12:31) is one of Jesus's best-known and most often-quoted sayings. Of course, we might not always love or even like our neighbours, whether living on the same street or knowing them at work, through church or elsewhere. However, most of us probably feel comfortable with the 'love your neighbour' part of Jesus's words: thinking of others, being kind to people. 'Yes, I can do that', we might say.

But what about, 'as yourself'? To have love for ourselves in the same way as we love others? That is more tricky. As Christians, ones who are encouraged to put others first, we might feel less comfortable with the concept of loving ourselves, as if it is somehow selfish or even sinful. Such discomfort has, over the years, been influenced by the Church's teaching which conveys a message that has often focussed on our sins and ensuring we remain humble, not being proud or boasting about who we are—let alone loving ourselves. There can even be a degree of 'guilt' associated with thinking about anything that could be seen as self-centred. Added to that, rather than feel comfortable with our strengths, many of us focus on our weaknesses, mistakes and misjudgements: all the ways people do not like what we say or do; all the pain and hurt we have experienced or inflicted; all we do not like, let alone love, about ourselves.

Yet, there are good things about and within each one of us. They may be hard to focus on at times but they are there: the things we got right; what we are good at; the successes (they do not have to be showstoppers); the compliments we receive (even if we struggle to accept or believe them). God's love for each of us is not based on success and achievement: we do not have to prove anything to God. God loves each one of us no less than anyone else, complete with all the bits we do not like that much. Whether or not or, indeed, whatever we think about God, God loves us regardless.

This book explores how our love for ourselves stems from God's love for us. There are thoughts from different Church traditions and wider society, together with contributions from people who have provided more personal insights specifically for this publication.

I explore the background and context of Jesus's words; what it means (and what it does not mean) to have love for ourselves; and how we can love ourselves in a way that enables us to love our neighbour. This book also considers and offers some practical suggestions, and you may like to jot down your thoughts as you read. And yes, just like trying to love ourselves, the text wrestles with some of the trickier parts too, and no doubt may not cover every aspect you can think of!

# 1
# THE SECOND COMMANDMENT

Imagine the scene: the Temple in Jerusalem is a hive of activity. The money-changers and pigeon-sellers are swarming around potential customers like bees hunting for pollen. The buzz of conversation is all about the man who caused chaos the previous day. Turning over the tables and reprimanding those who had turned the Temple into 'a den of robbers' (Matt. 21:13).

And now, now he's back. What on earth is he going to do next?

It is Tuesday of what we now call Holy Week. Mark's Gospel tells us how the chief priests, scribes and elders challenge Jesus and question his authority.[1] As on so many occasions, Jesus's replies stir up confusion among his questioners. Not to be defeated, they send along some Pharisees and Herodians 'to trap him' followed by some Sadducees. But Jesus outwits them all.[2]

Mark then describes the more 'considered' approach of a scribe, one whom Matthew calls a lawyer. This man sees the other questioners arguing amongst themselves and, perhaps catching the eye of Jesus, goes over to him. 'Teacher, which commandment in the law is the greatest?' (Matt. 22:36) he asks. Like the others, this man draws upon a knowledge of the scriptures, laws and traditions which had shaped his way of life and belief. In his response, Jesus does the same, for he too is steeped in those teachings. Recalling words spoken by Moses soon after receiving the Ten Commandments, Jesus replies, 'The first is, "Hear, O Israel: the Lord our God, the Lord is one;[3] you shall love the Lord your God with all your heart,

---

[1] Mark 11:27–12:12.

[2] Mark 12:13–27.

[3] This is the beginning of what is called the 'Shema Prayer'.

and with all your soul, and with all your mind, and with all your strength"' (Mark 12:29–30 quoting Deut. 6:4–5). He then quotes Leviticus 19:18, describing it as the second commandment: 'You shall love your neighbour as yourself.' (Mark 12:31). A solitary verse which, were it not so important, could easily have been overlooked among the nine chapters of the 'Holiness Code'.

Rabbi Jamie Stolper explains:

> Leviticus chapters 17–26 is known as the Holiness Code. It contains mainly commandments whose goals are to infuse holiness into the people of Israel, just as God is holy. These commandments, particularly in chapter 19, for the first time make it clear that holiness is not just a property of the relationship between humans and God, but also between human beings and other human beings.[4]

Tom Wright observes that Jesus's initial answer is apparently a conventional one:

> The Shema prayer ... was already central to Jewish devotion. Wholehearted love of God, and of one's neighbour as oneself, is basic to what God had in mind in giving the Torah. We also note the difference between the unreserved love of God and the measured love of neighbour—no more, but no less, than one loves one's own sinful self.[5]

Note those words: 'no more, but no less than one loves one's own sinful self': love your neighbour as yourself.

Mark's record of Jesus's word for love on this occasion uses the Greek ἀγάπη—agápé. Agape is the highest form of love: the Divine Love that comes from God. 'To love the neighbour cannot mean that one gives all of oneself to the neighbour; to do so would be an act of idolatry', writes Victor McCracken, Assistant Professor of Theology and Ethics at Abilene Christian University, Texas:

---

[4] Jamie Stolper, 'Love Your Neighbor As Thyself ואהבת לרעך כמוך Leviticus 19:18', *Sefaria* (6 December 2020), tinyurl.com/ 7283-0423-9-13.

[5] Tom Wright, *Twelve Months of Sundays Years A, B & C: Biblical Meditations on the Christian Year* (SPCK, 2012), Year B, 120–1.

> We love God because God first loved us: agape toward the neighbour, in contrast, enjoins that we love our neighbour even when our neighbour refuses to reciprocate ... To love my neighbour agapaically requires that I recognize my neighbour as one who is irreducibly valued.[6]

Having heard Jesus's response and, unlike the previous questioners, this scribe, this lawyer, gets it. 'You are right, Teacher' (Mark 12:32) he says, and goes on to quote words from Isaiah 45:5–6 in affirmation that what Jesus has said is more important than anything else:

> '... you have truly said that "he is one, and besides him there is no other"; and "to love him with all the heart, and with all the understanding, and with all the strength", and "to love one's neighbour as oneself",—this is much more important than all whole burnt-offerings and sacrifices.' (Mark 12:32–3)

With this response—and note the similarities with his encounter with another prominent Jew, Nicodemus the pharisee[7]—Jesus recognizes that, in his understanding, this particular scribe is 'not far from the kingdom of God' (Mark 12:34). Just a few days later, he will speak not dissimilar words to a criminal hanging on a cross next to him 'Truly I tell you, today you will be with me in Paradise.' (Luke 23:43).

This second commandment, as Jesus calls it, is also reminiscent of other teaching: 'Do to others as you would have them do to you.' (Luke 6:31; Matt. 7:12). Often referred to as 'The Golden Rule', its original form predates Christ and versions can be found in several ancient philosophies. It is a familiar tenet and we have all done or said things to others which we would not like done or said to us. All of us have also been on the receiving end of the words and actions of others which we would not wish to inflict on someone else.

---

[6] Victor McCracken, 'Mark 12:28–24, Theological Perspective', in *Feasting on the Word Year B, Volume 4: Season After Pentecost*, eds. David L. Bartlett and Barbara Brown Taylor (Westminster John Knox Press, 2013), 262.

[7] John 3:1–21.

## *A non-issue*

Writing some fifty years ago, Walter Trobisch asserted: 'It is an established fact that nobody is born with the ability to love himself.'[8] He quotes fellow German psychotherapist Guido Groeger:

> Self-love is either acquired or non-existent. The one who does not acquire it or acquires it insufficiently either is not able to love others at all or to love them only insufficiently.[9]

Both are arguable points but they open the door to our consideration of the trickier aspects of loving ourselves. Indeed, many would argue with both Trobisch and Groeger and say that we definitely are born self-centered and instinctively behave in such a manner—as those who have or care for babies and children might well testify.

On another related tack, one of the personal contributors to this book, Martin, wrote: 'I think this [loving ourselves] is a non-issue. I don't think Jesus ever intended to promote loving ourselves. I think he assumed, rightly, that we do that anyway.'[10]

This raises the question of whether Jesus's life and teaching instil within us the knowledge of God's love to the extent that we would understand it is also love we have for ourselves. Or did Jesus's insight into the human condition recognize we would be full of our own ego and pride in any case?

The trickier aspects of this topic can be found in other places too. As I mentioned above, to 'love your neighbour as yourself' is a verse which is often quoted and, just as often, misquoted. Anglican priest Revd Oliver Harrison writes:

> [The] Bible does *not* say 'Love your neighbour as you love yourself' but 'Love your neighbour as yourself'. You can't love yourself—not

---

[8] Walter Trobisch, *Love Yourself: Self-Acceptance and Depression* (Editions Trobisch, 1976), 2.
[9] Guido Groeger quoted in Trobisch, *Love Yourself*, 3.
[10] Name changed. Personal e-mail to the author, 21 August 2024.

really. Love requires more than one person: one to love and one to be loved. Love flows between people—plural. Two or more. Love by definition requires a lover and a beloved, a subject and an object, a giver and a receiver.

The misquoting of that passage has consequences. It is used as the prooftext for a whole industry of self-love. 'Love yourself' has become a mantra, a maxim, a moral imperative. A popular saying is 'If you don't love yourself how are you going to love anyone else?' Mostly people don't need any excuse or opportunity to 'love' themselves—to be selfish and mean and greedy and lazy and so on.[11]

Like Trobisch, albeit somewhat contradicting him, Harrison's comments are provocative and, both implicitly and explicitly, in tune with some of the Church's teaching that has also treated promoting such love for oneself as being self-centred, narcissistic and sinful. He is not alone in his concerns.

As I mentioned in the Introduction, I am grateful to those people who contacted me to offer their thoughts and experiences. Many of these referred to the somewhat more complex and trickier aspects of this theme of loving ourselves. Here, Laura describes her conundrum:

> This little piece has been more difficult to write than I ever thought it would be. I had to talk to a couple of good friends about how they saw me and what I consider, quite often, to be my self-centred habits and over-blown self love. Happily, and somewhat to my relief, they both confirmed what they see is not so much 'self love' but 'self confidence'.
> I can see now that confidence might easily be confused with being conceited and full of yourself and there are most definitely times when having too much confidence can become a problem.[12]

Another contribution, from Jake, showed how some people don't even consider the idea of self-love:

---

[11] Oliver Harrison, 'No, You Should Not Love Your Neighbour "as you love yourself"', *Psephizo* (27 April 2020) tinyurl.com/7283-0423-9-1 (accessed 26 Mar 2025).

[12] Name changed. Personal e-mail to the author, 22 December 2024.

> I have thought about one aspect of this for a few years. I never say to myself 'I love you'. I never even think it. My love of myself is shown in dressing appropriately for the weather conditions, seeing a Doctor when I am not well, taking medication, sleeping etc. My love for myself is entirely practical rather than emotional.[13]

And as Jenny observed in her email, a factor in our ability and inability to love ourselves that we should consider is that of self-criticism:

> I have been a perfectionist for most of my life and this has made it really hard to love myself. I am very hard on myself when I make mistakes and see my failures, as most perfectionists are. I am critical and judgemental of myself. And also unforgiving. This had led to me feeling a lot of shame for not living up to my own expectations. I am getting better at not being such a perfectionist, but it's not been easy.[14]

A related experience, by Joy, suggests that:

> In order to understand that you view your willingness to serve others instead (or better) than you would yourself—you first have to recognise and accept that you do that. I was at least 40 before I even realised that was what I was doing. Though random, the realisation occurred when I was asked by a manager what my life motto was; and the only thing I could say was 'A brownie guide thinks of others before herself and does a good turn every day'. He rephrased that and said it should be 'as well as myself'.[15]

Another contributor, Susan, highlighted further complexities in the understanding of Jesus's words and the realities of modern-day demands and living:

> I think lots of Christian believers find themselves in the role of martyr. Caring for and loving others before themselves. It can be a behaviour that grows into an unhealthy person and eventually a frustrated Christian. But then if we think to the times when Jesus took himself away to pray, then wasn't that self care? Self love? To spend time

---

[13] Name changed. Personal e-mail to the author, 28 August 2024.
[14] Name changed. Personal e-mail to the author, 27 August 2024.
[15] Name changed. Personal e-mail to the author, 23 August 2024.

alone with His maker? To draw boundaries and discover themselves through God.[16]

However, it is possible to develop a positive approach to having love for oneself from an early age, as Sarah demonstrates:

> When I was growing up, this was always a phrase [my Mum] would use: 'I'm OK, You're OK'—especially if I was worried about a particular encounter with someone, e.g. interviews or tricky conversations. So from a very young age, what this taught me to think about myself was, 'I am an OK person; I try to be kind and make the right choices, and so do most other people I will meet'. In this sense, being 'OK' was about assuming the best about myself and others. And so I suppose that, along with my Christian belief that God made us all and calls us 'very good', undergirds how I see myself and others. Just as I see others as worthy of love, so I see myself as worthy of love.[17]

For Victor McCracken, Jesus's words also raise another possibility, although he acknowledges that, like my contributors, not all theologians think the same way:

> Could self-love be analogous to the love that is due to our neighbour? A prominent stream of the Christian theological tradition treats self-love as the opposite of agape, often associating self-love with human pride and self-seeking. … The reasonable sense of Mark 12:31 suggests that self-love is both natural and justifiable within certain limits. For Aquinas it is not self-love per se that is the root of human sin but rather inordinate love of self that turns what is natural—the love that is naturally due oneself—into an acquisitive form of idolatry. To love one's neighbour as oneself suggests that there are continuities between natural self-love and agape. It is by knowing how to love oneself that one learns how to properly love the neighbour.[18]

Most of us feel significant diffidence about self-love, as Phil wrote in his contribution:

---

[16] Name changed. Reply to author's post on Facebook, 31 August 2024.
[17] Name changed. Personal e-mail to the author, 7 November 2024.
[18] McCracken, in *Feasting on the Word Year B*, 262.

I get the instinctive difficulty, caution, hesitancy re 'loving ourselves', essential as that may be if we're to love anyone else, for 'you can't give what you don't have'. But I wonder if the difficulty pivots on what we mean by 'love' and how strongly that's conflated in our modern culture with romantic idealism. I'm aware of various reframings and redefinitions in allied areas that reconsider 'love'. For example, seeing it as a verb rather than a noun. It's not something you have or don't have, get or don't get but something you do.[19]

In her book, *The Spiritual Life*, Evelyn Underhill put it like this:

> [We spend our lives] conjugating three verbs: to Want, to Have and to Do ... [keeping us in] perpetual unrest, forgetting that none of these verbs have any ultimate significance, except in so far as they are transcended by and included in the fundamental verb to Be.[20]

We are now getting to see some of the pieces of the jigsaw. But what is the picture on the cover of the box? Oliver Harrison gives us a clue: 'Get the quotation right—"Love your neighbour as yourself"—and it becomes beautiful and difficult and wonderful and risky.'[21]

---

[19] Name changed. Reply to author's post on Facebook, 24 August 2024.
[20] Evelyn Underhill, *The Spiritual Life* (Church Publishing Incorporated, 1985), 20.
[21] Harrison, 'No, You Should Not Love Your Neighbour "as you love yourself"'.

# 2
# WHAT IS LOVE?

What is this love which is beautiful and difficult and wonderful and risky? There are probably as many answers to that question as there are people, so let us consider some further thoughts and interpretations.

I have already mentioned agape, which is one of the four kinds of love indicated in the Greek used in the Bible. These are:

*Eros*: sensual or romantic love.

*Storge*: family love, the affectionate bond that develops naturally between parents and children, and brothers and sisters.

*Phileo*: love for and from fellow humans; care, respect and compassion for other people.

*Agape*: Divine Love that comes from God; perfect, unconditional, sacrificial, and pure.

Expressions of love based on eros are felt most strongly within loving, sexual relationships and are not experienced by everyone. Arguably, the vast majority of people will both give and receive love which stems from storge and phileo, although these are not without complications.

In that best-known passage about love, 1 Corinthians 13, Paul uses agape in describing the gift and meaning of love:

> [4] Love is patient; love is kind; love is not envious or boastful or arrogant [5] or rude. It does not insist on its own way; it is not irritable or resentful; [6] it does not rejoice in wrongdoing, but rejoices in the truth. [7] It bears all things, believes all things, hopes all things, endures all things.   (1 Cor. 13:4–7)

We can read those verses as ones which describe the pinnacle of loving our neighbour. Try substituting the word 'love' (and thus 'it') with your name.

I appreciate that may have felt a somewhat awkward and uncomfortable exercise. Be assured that all of us have trouble reaching the summit but Paul's steps are worthy ones to take as we climb. Let us take a moment to reflect on these beautiful and wonderful words and consider a difficult and risky aspect to them. How do they read when it comes to applying that love to ourselves?

Verse 4: Am I patient and kind to myself? Am I boastful and arrogant about myself or behave in ways to make others envious?

Verse 5: Am I rude to myself—by being too self-critical or calling myself 'stupid' or 'horrible' or some such? Does my insistence on having my own way stop others showing love to me? Would irritability or resentfulness with myself (about those aspects of my life which I don't like, for example) be better served by trying to accept those difficulties?

Verse 6: Am I constantly, as the NIV (among others) puts it, 'keeping a record' of the things I get wrong?[22] Why not rejoice in the truths, the good things about the person I am?

Verse 7: In modern parlance, one could call the traits shown in verse 7 'resilience'. Resilience is something that we develop over time and not something we can just 'switch on', as it is often portrayed. Love for ourselves takes time.

Asking such difficult and risky questions of ourselves helps with our inner awareness of who we are and who God created us to be. That can, in turn, enable us to have a better understanding of how to be kind, even to love, the person we are—with consequent benefits for the love of our neighbour also. Loving ourselves is not putting ourselves first above absolutely everything and everyone else, but having sufficient self-care in place that we are able to love our neighbour(s) in a way that is beneficial to them and not diminishing of ourselves.

---

[22] 1 Corinthians 13:5. Also Psalms 130:3 and 69:27; Job 14:16; Hosea 13:12.

## *A balancing act*

We live in a society where we are desperate to feel valued, heard and seen for who we are. We all want to feel loved in some way or other—be that in person or 'virtually' through social media. We might strive for that love through what we do or how much we earn. And yet, for example, we can work all the hours God sends only to find that we never spend any of them with the people we love and who love us. Over the years, I've seen far too many people working so hard to prove themselves to other people (and themselves) that they have become unable to love others and, consequently, unable to love themselves: putting everything in to everything only to be left with nothing for anything.

None of us are as important as we might think we are or want to be. Take me, for example: during a nearly forty-year career, I helped thousands of people to find or remain in employment, used to run an international mental health initiative and was appointed an MBE as a result. In the latter years, the people I worked alongside did what I asked them to (on the whole). I was seen, heard and valued for that work. Does that make me more valuable than others? No, of course not.

Similarly, we can also feel that we are not as important as other people. Indeed, since I retired from that work in 2018, along has come change and plenty of questions about who I am now. No longer am I someone who is as widely known or recognized for what I do. No longer do people always agree with me or do what I ask them to do. Filling the time now takes more effort. Levels of confidence fluctuate. Isolation is an unwelcome companion at times. As an author, and a non-bestselling one at that, and with low levels of podcast and social media 'likes', it is very easy to measure myself against those who are more successful. Does all that make me less important than others? No, of course not.

Loving ourselves means being realistic about who we are and not comparing ourselves to others. Theodore Roosevelt is credited with saying, 'Comparison is the thief of joy'. Or as fellow-American, the novelist

Anne Lamott put it, 'Try not to compare your insides to other people's outsides.'[23] St John Berchmans SJ wrote: 'Our true worth does not consist in what human beings think of us. What we really are consists in what God knows us to be.'[24] I do not believe God demands as much from us as we often think he does. The love of God means that God has realistic expectations of the person we are. Therefore, loving ourselves also means having realistic expectations of who we are. Loving ourselves is a matter of balance. For through God's love for us, we are all far more important than we think we are.

## *Telling our story*

As part of this balancing act, loving ourselves is also about the narrative we carry within us. Many of us live in the shadows or the impact of events, actions and words of the past—be they our own or those of others. Peter Scazzero describes this as our 'shadow side':

> Your shadow is the accumulation of untamed emotions, less-than-pure motives and thoughts that, while largely unconscious, strongly influence and shape your behaviours. It is the damaged but mostly hidden version of who you are.[25]

There may be very painful things which have pushed aside the love we might have for ourselves. Many people identify themselves according to their shadows and situations, subsequently losing their sense of who they really are—to the extent of becoming someone they do not even like, let alone love. At this point their sense of identity is defined almost totally by the situation and not the person they actually are.

---

[23] Anne Lamott, '12 Truths I Learned from Life and Writing', *TED talks* (April 2017), tinyurl.com/7283-0423-9-5 (accessed 26 Mar 2025). The Roosevelt quote originates with the stoic philosopher Seneca.

[24] Quoted in 'Saints: Saint John Berchmans', *Catholic Tradition* (undated) tinyurl.com/7283-0423-9-11 (accessed 9 January 2025).

[25] Peter Scazzero, *The Emotionally Healthy Leader* (Zondervan, 2015), 55.

One of the contributors referred to earlier, Laura, reflected on a period of depression following the death of her mother, an experience which challenged her sense of identity:

> What I do know is that I look back on that time—and some others—with huge gratitude because I learned so much and came back stronger. Persuading those who are at rock bottom is hard work especially if it seems that no-one around you is able to love you either.[26]

We might also feel a degree of shame for past actions, words or other damaging aspects of life. Such feelings can also affect us deeply. Brené Brown describes such occasions as 'shame attacks' and offers this advice in tackling them:

> Yes, I want to hide, but the way to fight shame and to honour who we are is by sharing our experience with someone who has earned the right to hear it—someone who loves us, not despite our vulnerabilities, but because of them.

She goes on to suggest that we are to talk to ourselves in the way we

> would talk to someone I really love and whom I am trying to comfort in the midst of a meltdown: You're okay. You're human—we all make mistakes. I've got your back. Normally during a shame attack we talk to ourselves in ways we would NEVER talk to people we love and respect.[27]

We can't change the events of the past (nor of the present in some cases) but we can change our response to them. Loving yourself sometimes also involves changing the narrative. 'Instead of thinking "I should have known that" and beating yourself up about it', writes Elim Pentecostal pastor and author Simon Lawton, 'turn it in to something you have learned and realized for the future.'[28]

---

[26] Name changed. Personal e-mail to the author, 22 December 2024.

[27] Brené Brown, *Daring Greatly: How the Courage to Be Vulnerable Transforms the Way We Live, Love, Parent, and Lead* (Penguin, 2012), 80 (author's emphasis).

[28] Simon Lawton, 'Don't Focus on the Waves', Instagram post (22 August 2024), https://www.instagram.com/simonlawton/ (accessed 22 August 2024).

Of course, that takes time and effort—as most loving does. If we've been living with the same narrative for years, it will take a long time to rewrite it and we may need help to do so. Seeking help is itself all part of loving ourselves. Seeking help is a sign of strength and not the sign of weakness or failure as some, perhaps even including ourselves, believe it to be, as contributor Jenny explained:

> I am learning to believe who I am in [God]. A place where my identity is found and that helps too. Something else that helps is making time to show myself self-compassion. We can find it easier to show compassion to others than we do to ourselves.[29]

Activist and mental health campaigner Patrick Regan also writes about the importance of self-compassion: '[It] isn't taking the easy way out, it's giving ourselves the kindness we need so that we're able to be kind to others.'[30] Bishop John Stroyan observes that:

> Our weaknesses, our fallibilities, far from being an obstacle to God's life and work in and through us, are, if acknowledged before God, the very raw material of his transforming grace.[31]

Many of us carry what Walter Trobisch refers to as 'a misconception about Christian modesty and humility'.[32] It is all right to feel good about ourselves; it is not selfish or self-indulgent. Loving ourselves is the ability to look in the mirror and to like, to love, the person we see. To love ourselves as we are because God first loved us.[33] Bishop Andrew Rumsey put it like this: 'If we want to be at home in the world, we need first to be at home to ourselves.'[34] Or as Trobisch wrote: 'We must learn to let ourselves be loved.'[35]

---

[29] Name changed. Personal e-mail to the author, 27 August 2024.
[30] Patrick Regan, *Honesty over Silence: It's OK Not to be OK* (SPCK, 2024), 99.
[31] John Stroyan, *Turned by Divine Love: Starting again with God and with Others* (Bible Reading Fellowship, 2019), 43.
[32] Trobisch, *Love Yourself*, 20.
[33] 1 John 4:19.
[34] Andrew Rumsey, *English Grounds: A Pastoral Journey* (SCM Press, 2023), 118.

Loving ourselves can be like nurturing a plant: acknowledging that which is difficult, weeping over it, and using those tears to enable growth to take place—growth rooted in the love of God. Loving ourselves does not mean that we have to be perfect, nor does it mean getting everything right. If we believe we have to be perfect, we diminish both the need for God and for the love of God in our lives. If we think we have to be perfect then are we effectively saying to God, I don't need you?

---

[35] Trobisch, *Love Yourself*, 19.

# 3
# KNOWING GOD'S LOVE

God first loved us; loved us before we were born and every single moment since. By knowing we are loved by God, deep down, we can be fully enabled to pass on that love to our neighbour. It is through that love for us that we can also love ourselves.

Of course, God's love can be conveyed to and received by others without the need for us (as potential channels of that love) to love ourselves deeply. Indeed, many would say that happens in any case. Many people do not love themselves particularly well or deep down yet still convey love for their neighbour. Love for our neighbour can at times feel far more effective and generous than such feelings for ourselves.

Yet if we are to love our neighbour as ourself, think how much more deeply God's love would be demonstrated to and received by others if we ourselves know the depth of the love God has for us—a depth which reaches right into, and arises from within our hearts.

## *Purity of heart*

So far we have looked at aspects of the focus of this book through our thoughts and those of others, using our minds to explore this topic in a largely objective manner. What lies within our hearts is perhaps not so easy to define and requires more subjective language.

Some common phrases are helpful in unpacking this further: 'From the bottom of my heart.' 'My heart's not in it.' 'A broken heart.' Or even 'Be still, my beating heart.' We might find, like John Wesley, that our heart is 'strangely warmed' by particular spiritual or other encounters.[36] We can feel an inner emotional excitement or fear at the anticipation or

---

[36] Journal entry for 24 May 1738.

presence of a particular person. We may have a 'heavy heart' in the knowledge of, or encounter with, sadness and grief.

The concept of having a 'pure heart' has been recognized and valued since Old Testament times:

> Create in me a clean heart, O God, and put a new and right spirit within me. (Ps. 51:10)
>
> Truly God is good to the upright, to those who are pure in heart. (Ps. 73:1)

And in the New Testament:

> Blessed are the pure in heart, for they will see God. (Matt. 5:8)
>
> But the aim of such instruction is love that comes from a pure heart, a good conscience, and sincere faith. (1 Tim. 1:5)
>
> Now that you have purified your souls by your obedience to the truth so that you have genuine mutual love, love one another deeply from the heart. (1 Pet. 1:22)

We can also learn from the teaching and experience of the Desert Mothers and Fathers. After the Roman Emperor Constantine embraced Christianity and legalized its practice in 313 AD, there was a cultural shift. 'After 3 centuries of "being homeless in the world" Christians began to find themselves in favour, rather than persecuted', wrote Trevor Miller; 'The result was confusion and bewilderment in those who had accepted themselves as aliens and strangers in this world.'[37] 'Their journey into the desert was a movement toward growing intentional awareness of God's presence and recognizing that worldly pleasures bring little long-term satisfaction', observed Christine Valters Paintner; 'Their aim was to experience God in each moment and activity by reducing their needs and committing themselves to the discipline of regular prayer and self-inquiry.'[38]

---

[37] Trevor Miller, 'Understanding Desert Monasticism' [talk transcript], *Northumbria Community* (17 June 2013), tinyurl.com/7283-0423-9-8 (accessed 26 Mar 2025).

[38] Christine Valters Paintner, 'The Desert Mothers and Fathers Showed all Life is Sacred', *U.S. Catholic*, 31 January 2020, tinyurl.com/7283-0423-9-14 (accessed 13 March 2025).

Living in the deserts of Egypt, Palestine, Syria, and Arabia in the fourth and fifth centuries AD, these ordinary Christians lived an ascetic lifestyle to follow God's call. Their spiritual practice influenced Western and Eastern Christianity through their focus on spiritual labours and nurturing purity of heart. Mark Kutolowski wrote:

> … they came to recognize inner obstacles that could be identified and removed through spiritual disciplines like prayer, fasting, and vigils. Simply removing these inner blockages allowed for the natural radiance of God's light, life, and light to shine through their hearts and illumine their entire beings. … The work of purifying the heart is the spiritual journey from who we 'think' we are to our deeper self, hidden with Christ in God. It is this deeper self that is capable of both attaining inner peace and of being a gift and a blessing to others.[39]

If all that sounds too unattainable let us break it down a bit with the help of two monastics, one a very early one, and the other from the present day. Born in Constantinople (now Istanbul in Turkey), Maximus the Confessor (580–662) was highly educated and mixed with the elite. Appointed as a secretary to the Emperor he left this privileged lifestyle after just three years to enter a monastery. His work *Four Centuries on Love*[40] is one of those reflected upon by Nicholas Worssam SSF, a present-day monastic in the Franciscan Order. He summarizes Maximus's definition of love as being the following sequence:

> Faith in God → fear of God → self-control → patience & forbearance → hope in God → dispassion → love

Worssam explains how 'Faith in God is one of the "three theological virtues" spoken of by Paul in 1 Cor. 13:13: "faith, hope, and love abide, these

---

[39] Mark Kutolowski, 'Purifying the Heart: What the Desert Elders Can Teach Us about Healing Our World—and Ourselves' (1 February 2021), tinyurl.com/7283-0423-9-4 (accessed 9 January 2025).

[40] Also known as *Four Hundred Texts on Love*. Maximus the Confessor, *Centuries on Love*, trans. in G. Berthold, *Maximus Confessor: Selected Writings*, Classics of Western Spirituality (Paulist Press, 1985), 35–98.

three; and the greatest of these is love." Fear of God is referring not to a debilitating anxiety, but to a sense of reverence at the awe-inspiring mystery of God.'[41] Worssam goes on to describe self-control as regulating unhelpful impulses, such as pausing before responding and acting rather than reacting: '[self-control] is itself a kind of patience and forbearance, directed towards oneself as much as others.'[42] These all lead to the development and experience of hope in God, another of the theological virtues.

One could view the next stage of dispassion as being unemotional or emotionally uninvolved, so dispassion is perhaps a strange word to use when we are talking about love. But to quote Maximus, 'We cannot attain lasting possession of such love while we are still attached to anything worldly.'[43] In other words, we are to endeavour to put aside worldly distractions and the confusion that emotions can bring. 'The virtue of dispassion', Worssam writes, 'carries the meaning of equanimity, reintegration and spiritual freedom.'[44]

Acknowledging these views could be difficult for modern-day readers, Worssam reminds us that dispassion was translated into Latin by John Cassian (360–435) as *puritas cordis*: purity of heart. 'As such', Worssam explains, 'it is that by which God is seen and known (Matt. 5:8) and is described here by Maximus as the immediate precursor to love.'[45] In order to love our neighbour and ourselves effectively, a degree of dispassion (e.g. calmness, detachment, objectivity) is needed.

It is important to recognize and acknowledge that our experience of love—for neighbour, for self and for God—exists at whatever stage we might have reached in the sequence alluded to by Maximus, and is not solely the 'destination'. The flowchart opposite could also be drawn

---

[41] Nicholas Alan Worssam SSF, *In the Stillness, Waiting: Christian Origins of the Prayer of the Heart* (Canterbury Press, 2024), 139.
[42] Idem, 138.
[43] Maximus, *Centuries on Love*, I.1.
[44] Worssam, *In the Stillness, Waiting*, 139.
[45] Ibid.

as a circle to demonstrate that, as we experience and receive love, it builds up (or goes deeper into) our faith in God.

Even that could be a circle within a circle: our whole faith journey and life are encircled by love.

By nurturing this love, and thus purity of heart, within us through the continuous exploration of the various stages outlined above, we receive and experience love at ever deeper levels within our hearts. And that in turn enables us to love our neighbour as ourselves.

Søren Kierkegaard wrote 'purity of heart is to will one thing'. Reflecting on this and the teaching of Jesus, Richard Rohr observes:

> It's quite clear that Jesus was entirely single-hearted. His life was all about doing the will of the One who sent him, the One he loved above all. To Jesus, it was that simple. As we grow spiritually, our lives become more and more centred and simple. There are only a few things that matter, and eventually really only one.[46]

Now, you might say, 'Well, that's all very good for people like the Desert Mothers and Fathers, Kierkegaard and Richard Rohr. But this is me!'

---

[46] Richard Rohr, 'Purity of Heart', *Center for Action and Contemplation* (28 April 2024), tinyurl.com/7283-0423-9-10 (accessed 26 Mar 2025). Søren Kierkegaard, *Purity of Heart is to Will One Thing*, trans. Douglas van Steere (Harper, 1938).

# 4
# INTENTIONAL ATTENTION

So, what does this purity of heart mean in the beautiful and difficult and wonderful and risky things of day-to-day life? We will explore this on two fronts. In this chapter, the spiritual approaches we can take and, in the one that follows, the practical, day-to-day aspects of showing love for ourselves.

'Purity of heart is about seeking union with God for no other reason than who God *is*, and not what God *can do*', writes Benedictine monastic, Br Anselm Philip King-Lowe OSB. He suggests that one way of nurturing purity of heart is found through contemplative prayer: 'Contemplative prayer is an act of letting go of the things that weigh us down, of what keeps us from a search for that union with God with a purity of heart.'[47]

Elsewhere he writes, 'It is through a life of prayer that we seek union with God praying for a purity of heart. A heart that wants God and nothing more.'[48] As familiar as it may sound, prayer is the fundamental and solid foundation of every aspect of our lives: including that of nurturing love for ourselves and our neighbour. As Worssam reminds us: 'Every path is unique, and each one is adapted to the ability and daily realities of a person's life.'[49]

---

[47] Br Anselm Philip King-Lowe OSB, 'Reflection on Be Not Far Away', *Simple Reflections for a Deeper Spiritual Life* (10 April 2020), tinyurl.com/7283-0423-9-2 (accessed 26 Mar 2025).

[48] Br Anselm Philip King-Lowe OSB, 'Reflection on God is My Portion', *Simple Reflections for a Deeper Spiritual Life* (26 June 2020), tinyurl.com/7283-0423-9-3 (accessed 26 Mar 2025).

[49] Worssam, *In the Stillness, Waiting*, 156.

Sometimes, our prayers are conscious, said in specific times we set aside. At other times they may be the result of a 'holy nudge' or take the form of simply talking to God in the way we might to another person. Our prayers may also be without words when we live with an awareness of God (even when held lightly or in retrospect). Indeed, we might recognize God's presence, action and love in the events of life as they actually happen or as we look back, whether later in the hour, day, week or when the years have gone by. Nurturing purity of heart and union with God includes an approach of deepening and increasing our awareness of God by paying intentional attention, as much as we are able, within the day-to-day realities of our lives. 'The God who meets us personally at a particular time and in a particular place', writes John Stroyan, 'is also the God who is with us at all times and in all places.'[50]

## Come as you are

There is no single, right way to pray or to read the Bible, and it is helpful to find ways of doing both which suit you as the person God has made you to be and are becoming. Such approaches may include using structured liturgy or free-flowing extemporary prayers—or both. It may be having set quiet times or praying as and when you feel nudged or inspired—or both. If someone else finds daily Bible reading notes helpful then that's great but don't worry if they do not suit you. If someone else does not find structured liturgy helpful that does not mean to say that you won't. What other people do is of no consequence—apart from negative ones. If we continue to try to be like someone else (or what we perceive them to be), then we will always have a sense of failure and inadequacy.

There are many practical ways of enriching this aspect of faith. We might use the daily Bible notes mentioned above, or online resources and Apps such as 'Pray as you Go' and Common Worship 'Daily Prayer'. Using

---

[50] Stroyan, *Turned by Divine Love*, 16.

an icon as a 'window on prayer' or simple focal points such as a candle or holding a cross can help concentrate the mind as we pay intentional attention to God. Practices such as listening to worship music, *lectio divina*, centring prayer or Ignatian spiritual exercises may be helpful.

If you are not used to long periods of silence in prayer or meditation, you are not alone. Distracting thoughts are quite normal too. If being in silence is new (or even uncomfortable), just try it for two or three minutes to begin with. Do the same again for a few days and gradually lengthen the time (not that the time is important, of course). And don't force yourself to be holy—or as Thomas Merton put it, 'Don't seek self-indulgent serenity.'[51] Don't worry if 'nothing happens'. Mother Maribel CSMV wrote, 'Silence is not a thing we make, it is something into which we enter. It is always there.'[52]

Whether formal or informal, structured or unstructured, spoken or silent, come as you are. And may the approaches taken be ones which enable a deeper union with God. That in itself will deepen the awareness of God's love for you, your love for yourself and that which you hold for your neighbours.

I turn to the words of another contributor to this book, Jenny, to sum up this chapter about nurturing purity of heart and paying intentional attention to God:

> What I have found helpful in learning to love myself is spending time in God's presence and learning how he feels about me. That he loves me because he is love and not because of what I can or can't do.[53]

---

[51] Attributed to Thomas Merton, source unknown.
[52] From the notes for guests staying at Mucknell Abbey, Worcestershire.
[53] Name changed. Personal e-mail to the author, 27 August 2024.

# 5
# DAY TO DAY

During the last couple of decades, awareness of personal wellbeing and self-care has become more prominent in Western society. The term 'wellbeing' covers several aspects of the way people feel about their lives, including their jobs and their relationships with the people around them. Encompassed within this heading are physical self-care aspects such as diet, exercise, alternative therapies, and other ways to look after the body.

This increased awareness has ridden in tandem with improved understanding about mental health and mental ill-health. The two are different, by the way: it is common to hear people use the term 'mental health' when in fact referring to 'mental ill-health', such as depression, anxiety and more severe conditions such as psychosis.

The World Health Organization defines 'mental health' as

> a state of mental well-being that enables people to cope with the stresses of life, realize their abilities, learn well and work well, and contribute to their community.[54]

That is a very positive definition. Looking after our mental health helps us both to love ourselves (realize our ambitions; cope with stress) and to love our neighbours in the broadest sense (learn well and work well; make a contribution to community).

As I have mentioned the word 'stress', I'll take a brief detour on our journey. There is no such thing as 'good stress'. We all need a degree of pressure to feel good and function well. But stress is the feeling we experience when we are under too much pressure and the demands

---

[54] 'Mental Health', *World Health Organization* (19 December 2019), tinyurl.com/7283-0423-9-6 (accessed 26 Mar 2025).

outweigh our personal resources, capacity and strength. And that is not a good thing.

Stress can show itself in many ways. Here are some examples (this is not an exhaustive list):

Physically—higher blood pressure; eczema; faster heartbeat; sexual dysfunction.

Behaviourally—being more irritable; sleep problems; biting nails; crying; drinking more alcohol.

Psychologically—feeling overwhelmed; unable to make decisions; low mood; anxiousness, rushing.

Left unaddressed such symptoms may lead to other difficulties in our health and wellbeing—and sadly, I have seen that happen in far too many people. There are other symptoms and it is useful to know your own responses and reactions during times of feeling stressed (we will return to looking after ourselves in such periods shortly).

Back then to our main route. In summary, 'wellbeing is about *feeling good* and *functioning well*'.[55] This is, in many respects, connected to other words of Jesus: ' I came that [you] may have life, and have it abundantly' (John 10:10)—a verse sometimes used as a way of encouraging people to look for hope, joy, satisfaction, wellness. But, being realistic, life will never be without difficulty and it is pointless to expect it to be so.

Author, broadcaster and priest Richard Coles put it something like this: life in all its fullness is about love, joy, fear, despair, grief, sadness and everything else we experience that is harsh and difficult. All are parts of this thing we call a liveable life. Taking the rough with the smooth. Knowing that in the river of life both rough and smooth waters exist side by side. This is life in all its fullness.[56]

---

[55] Jody Aked, et al., *Five Ways to Wellbeing: New Applications, New Ways of Thinking* (New Economics Foundation, 2008), 1 (my emphasis).

[56] Revd Richard Coles, paraphrased from an unscripted talk given at The Corn Exchange, Exeter, 15 November 2023.

Feeling good and functioning well is just one part of loving oneself—partly for its own sake but also in order that we might love our neighbour too. So how do we go about feeling good and functioning well? How do we, in very practical ways, love ourselves amidst daily stresses and pressures?

## *Being real*

You know how it is: work (or church) beckons and you don't feel well. The non-conscientious may 'throw a sickie'. The rest (arguably, most people) endure an internal struggle:

'Perhaps if I go in, I'll feel better—but what if I feel worse?'

'I really don't feel well enough but they can't manage without me. And there's so much that needs doing.'

'If I don't go, what will they think of me?'

'I'll let everyone down.'

And so it goes on. The tussle between loving ourselves and loving our neighbour … colleagues, customers and everyone else.

Other factors complicate this confusing aspect of daily life. Access to emails and working from home, while advantageous in many ways, have further developed an 'always on' mentality for many. What does that email sent outside what used to be described as 'normal working hours' say about our attitudes towards both our 'neighbour' (be they work colleague, vicar or committee member etc.) and to ourselves?

'They're working—should I be?'

'I'm working—why aren't they?'

Or maybe you're having a really tough time—dealing with such things as illness, bereavement, financial worries, loneliness, family or work problems, for example. You are at the end of your tether: the phone rings or a message pings—yet another demand. Do you say 'No' and preserve your own wellbeing? Or 'Yes' and help someone else?

It is all so reminiscent of the Parable of the Good Samaritan, isn't it? A story Jesus told to a lawyer who quoted those very verses from Deuteronomy and Leviticus which form the basis of the second commandment.[57] Do we walk by on the other side or stop and help?

Loving our neighbour as ourselves is not easy or straightforward, is it? So let us now consider some of the realities of day-to-day living and a few practical ways to nurture a balanced approach to showing love and care for ourselves. You may well be doing much of this already but it's worth giving ourselves the equivalent of an 'MOT' every so often…

*Physical self-care*

Looking after our body is crucial. Why not take some time to reflect on what you are eating and drinking; how are those necessities of human functioning helping to maintain your health and wellbeing? Regular exercise is also shown to be beneficial—whether it's walking, swimming, going to the gym or something less strenuous. If you have a limiting health condition then do what you can—for example, some chair exercises. What activities are helping maintain your physical wellbeing?

*Good sleep*

An uninterrupted eight hours of sleep is a pretty rare thing (only one in five people get at least that much).[58] Indeed, lots of people don't *need* eight hours, so we shouldn't get hung up on that number, when what is important is what is enough for each individual. Good sleep hygiene such as a regular bedtime routine helps: although any underlying causes of poor sleep (such as anxiety) may still need to be addressed. Rest isn't always restorative but getting to know our 'tired times' of the day can

---

[57] Luke 10:27.

[58] Matthew Smith, 'Three Quarters of Brits Get Less than Eight Hours Sleep', *YouGovUK* (17 January 2020), tinyurl.com/7283-0423-9-12 (accessed 26 Mar 2025).

help in dealing with demands and adjusting commitments accordingly. For example, we might also think of this in terms of whether we are a 'morning' or an 'afternoon' person.

## Relaxation, hobbies, fun!

Take a bit of time to reflect on how you relax or what hobbies or interests you have outside any work, study, family or volunteering commitments. Making time for the things we enjoy is a choice (even if we think it may not be). What gives you life in all its fullness?

## Time with family & friends

Whether we like it or not, humans are social beings. Hard as it is for some who are more introverted (and/or less confident), taking time to be with other people is an important way of overcoming isolation and loneliness, and is thus beneficial for our self-care.

## Does it have to be done right now?

We live in a 'this minute/last minute' society. On the one hand, there is an expectation for things to be done straight away. On the other, so much is attempted with little or no time left to complete it. There is so much pressure to expect and provide fast and immediate action (and also some distinctly poor role-modelling that goes with it). We have cultivated a society of unnecessary rushing. Taking time to think, to pray, to seek advice will, even if the speed of response is slower, often produce a much better and more fulfilling outcome.

## Should versus could

So many of us feel we must or should do things. Such unhelpful drivers can have a significant impact on our ability to truly love our neighbour, let alone ourselves. We can end up being driven—not called. Often attributed to Gerard Hughes SJ, but first coined by British psychiatrist Dr Frank Lake, the description of this attitude has been described as 'hardening of the oughteries'.[59] Perhaps instead of acting on our sometimes self-driven 'should' motivations, we might think about who else 'could'—and thus help develop gifts in other people at the same time, loving our neighbour too.

## Saying 'no'

'The problem is, Richard, one can't say "No" to people.' My reply took this person by surprise: 'What makes you think you're the right person to say "Yes"?'

Some people are, of course, very adept at saying 'No' (both negatively and positively!). But for many, doing so can feel uncomfortable and unloving towards their neighbour. We may feel a certain obligation to say 'Yes' to any request or demand. For some, this response, as alluded to by Susan, one of my contributors in Chapter One, is fed by being a martyr to the cause. A feeling that this is what is expected both by others and by ourselves. Yet, are we always the best person to say 'Yes'? Who else has the knowledge and the ability (and perhaps the time) to do so? So many situations are not helped by those who believe they are the best person to do it. The ability to say 'No' and signpost it to someone else is a sign of love for both our neighbour and ourself.

## Focus on strengths

Many people focus on their weaknesses and mistakes. It is fine to feel good about yourself and to recognize what God has placed within us for the benefit of others. Why not take some time to write down the things you are good at and the gifts God has given you? Alongside that,

---

[59] Frank Lake, *Clinical Theology: A Theological and Psychological Basis to Clinical Pastoral Care* (Darton, Longman & Todd, 1966), back cover.

we can be nurturing a thankful heart for who we are and asking for the strength of the Holy Spirit continually to stir up the gift of God that is in us.[60]

*Talking to someone*

Being honest with oneself and others is key to loving yourself. There are times to accept that we may need some help, to ask someone to provide a listening ear or advice. There is no shame in that, no shame in letting our neighbour show love for us.

## This is me

You might like to make a note of some of things you've noticed about yourself. What could you start (or stop) doing immediately or in the next couple of weeks or during the coming months? And who else could help you do some of it?

More often than not our love for someone else is, in part, based on the person they are, and that love will grow (or not) as we get to know them more. So it is that love for ourself is, in part, also based on who we are, and will grow (or not) as we get to know who we are. As well as those practical aspects of nurturing a balanced approach to showing love and care for ourselves, it is also worth thinking about what makes us the person we are. Who is the self we are loving? Such self-awareness was demonstrated by two of the contributors to this book. One, Joy, found a Drivers Questionnaire helpful.[61] Such tools help us

---

[60] See the Church of England liturgy for 'The Admission and Licensing of Readers', *Common Worship* (The Archbishops' Council 2007): 'Will you then, in the strength of the Holy Spirit, continually stir up the gift of God that is in you to make Christ known to all?'

[61] There are various versions in existence for example Kahler's Five Drivers, cited in 'Kahler's Drivers', *TURAS Learn: Quality Improvement Zone* ( 29 May 2025), https://learn.nes.nhs.scot/27427 (accessed 26 Mar 2025).

to understand what motivates (drives) our personality and approaches to life and others:

> 'Please others', 'Be perfect' and 'Be strong' drivers were very high. I have used [the questionnaire] with lots of people since and I think it is a good 'self awakening' tool. With hindsight, it really helped me to understand some of the things that made me think of others differently to me. You can only deal with things you know are there.[62]

While another, Sarah, used the Enneagram, a model of the human psyche that is constructed around a theory of nine interconnected personality types (numbered 1–9):[63]

> I have found the Enneagram a really helpful tool for self-understanding, and therefore also for accepting elements of who I am. For example, I identify as a '1', which is often referred to as the 'Perfectionist' type, which means in the pursuit of wanting things to be 'just right', I can be critical of myself, others and situations. While I don't see 'being a 1' as condoning my criticisms, I find it helpful to realize that it often comes from a place of seeking the best and the good. So the Enneagram has helped me accept elements of who I am, while always seeking to offer up to God those parts of me that still need to be reformed by his forgiveness and grace.[64]

So let us now consider some other aspects of what makes us the person we are—and I invite you to do so for yourself. There are no 'right' or 'wrong' answers—just those which are yours:

1. **What makes you you?** What do you like about yourself? What makes you feel good? What do you think other people like about you? Why not write these things down as a reminder.
2. **What do you do to keep being the person you are?** Write down those things that are helpful to do every day to help in feeling good

---

[62] Name changed. Personal e-mail to the author, 23 January 2024.
[63] It is often used in business management to analyze interpersonal dynamics in the workplace.
[64] Name changed. Personal e-mail to the author, 7 November 2024.

and functioning well (e.g. time to yourself or with others, a dog walk, watching TV, reading, prayer times, etc.). Add on what you like doing every so often (e.g. going to the theatre, concerts, sport, retreat, etc.).

3. **What do you notice when you are not feeling like the person you are?** We all have bad days or difficult times in life. In such times, some people become more irritable or develop a reactive health issue (e.g. eczema, headaches, sleep issues). Some experience mood changes. Sometimes we might find ourselves feeling stressed. What do you notice about the way you feel or behave when things aren't going well? Jot them down too.

So, having written down your responses, keep them in a place where they are easy to find. You can always go back to them and add or change as time goes on. Then, when there are those times when you notice those things which are not quite right (list 3), ask yourself: 'Have I stopped doing the things on list 2?' Doing this can help redress the balance and continue to nurture what makes you 'you' (list 1).

When considering some of these practicalities of dealing with the stresses and pressures of life, which can so often get in the way of showing love towards our ourselves, we can also bear in mind some words of the Irish poet and author John O'Donohue:

> Stress is a perverted relationship to time, so that rather than being a subject of your own time, you have become its target and victim, and time has become routine. So at the end of the day, you probably haven't had a true moment for yourself, to relax in and to just be.
>
> Dan Siegel, my friend, has this lovely meditation: you imagine the surface of the ocean is all restless, and then you slip down deep below the surface, where it's still and where things move slower.[65]

---

[65] John O'Donohue, speaking to Krista Tippet on a podcast, 'The Inner Landscape of Beauty' [transcript] (28 February 2008), tinyurl.com/7283-0423-9-9 (accessed 9 Jan 2025).

## *Loving yourself*

In some respects, loving yourself is about being in a loving relationship with yourself. 'Essentially, you are teaching others how to love you, by the way you love yourself', wrote Anya Meyerowitz,

> Self-love is an ongoing, daily practice. It is not a destination, it is a great adventure. It is not something we suddenly switch on one day and all of our problems are solved. It is something we work on every single day.[66]

Combining the practical aspects of looking after our wellbeing and the nurturing of purity of heart enables us not only to be in union with God, but also to receive God's love: a love which is indescribable. Receiving love from God means that God is giving us that love. It is God's love for us that is transformed into love which we have for ourselves as people made in the image of God and equipped for God's service. Knowing we are loved by God, deep down below the surface, enables us to show love for our neighbour and to have love for ourselves.

---

[66] Anya Meyerowitz, '10 Things that People who Love Themselves Do', *Red* (25 November 2019), tinyurl.com/7283-0423-9-7 (accessed 26 Mar 2025).

# SOURCES AND RESOURCES MENTIONED IN THE TEXT

## Books

Aked, Jody, et al., *Five Ways to Wellbeing: New Applications, New Ways of Thinking* (New Economics Foundation, 2008).

Brown, Brené, *Daring Greatly: How the Courage to Be Vulnerable Transforms the Way We Live, Love, Parent, and Lead* (Penguin, 2012).

Lake, Frank, *Clinical Theology: A Theological and Psychological Basis to Clinical Pastoral Care* (Darton, Longman & Todd, 1966).

Maximus the Confessor, *Centuries on Love*, trans. in G. Berthold, *Maximus Confessor: Selected Writings*, Classics of Western Spirituality (Paulist Press, 1985).

McCracken, Victor 'Mark 12:28–24, Theological Perspective', in *Feasting on the Word Year B, Volume 4: Season After Pentecost*, eds. David L Bartlett and Barbara Brown Taylor (Westminster John Knox Press, 2013).

Regan, Patrick, *Honesty over Silence: It's OK Not to be OK* (SPCK, 2024).

Rumsey, Andrew, *English Grounds: A Pastoral Journey* (SCM Press, 2023).

Scazzero, Peter, *The Emotionally Healthy Leader* (Zondervan, 2015).

Stroyan, John, *Turned by Divine Love: Starting again with God and with Others* (Bible Reading Fellowship, 2019).

Trobisch, Walter, *Love Yourself: Self-Acceptance and Depression* (Editions Trobisch, 1976).

Underhill, Evelyn, *The Spiritual Life* (Church Publishing Incorporated, 1985, new edition Morehouse Publishing, 2008).

Worssam, Nicholas Alan, SSF, *In the Stillness, Waiting: Christian Origins of the Prayer of the Heart* (Canterbury Press, 2024).

Wright, Tom, *Twelve Months of Sundays Years A, B & C: Biblical Meditations on the Christian Year* (SPCK, 2012).

## *Online*

In order to facilitate re-keying of lengthy website addresses, a short version of all long URLs has been provided using the web-alias service tinyurl.com. These links are used in the footnotes to the text, and are given below, following the full citation.

Harrison, Oliver, 'No, You Should Not Love Your Neighbour "as you love yourself"', *Psephizo* (27 April 2020), https://www.psephizo.com/biblical-studies/no-you-should-not-love-your-neighbour-as-you-love-yourself/ (accessed 26 Mar 2025).

    ☑ tinyurl.com/7283-0423-9-1

'Kahler's Drivers', *TURAS Learn: Quality Improvement Zone* (29 May 2025), ☑ https://learn.nes.nhs.scot/27427 (accessed 26 Mar 2025).

King-Lowe, Br Anselm Philip OSB, 'Reflection on Be Not Far Away', *Simple Reflections for a Deeper Spiritual Life* (10 April 2020), https://simplereflectionsforadeeperspirituallife.wordpress.com/2020/04/10/reflection-on-be-not-far-away/ (accessed 26 Mar 2025).

    ☑ tinyurl.com/7283-0423-9-2

King-Lowe, Br Anselm Philip OSB, 'Reflection on God is My Portion', *Simple Reflections for a Deeper Spiritual Life* (26 June 2020), https://simplereflectionsforadeeperspirituallife.wordpress.com/2020/06/26/reflection-on-god-is-my-portion/ (accessed 26 Mar 2025).

    ☑ tinyurl.com/7283-0423-9-3

Kutolowski, Mark, 'Purifying the Heart: What the Desert Elders Can Teach Us about Healing Our World—and Ourselves' (1 February 2021), https://www.metanoiavt.com/reflections/2021/2/1/purifying-the-heart, (accessed 9 Jan 2025).

    ☑ tinyurl.com/7283-0423-9-4

Lamott, Anne, '12 Truths I Learned from Life and Writing', *TED talks* (April 2017), https://www.ted.com/talks/anne_lamott_12_truths_i_learned_from_life_and_writing/transcript (accessed 26 Mar 2025).

    ☑ tinyurl.com/7283-0423-9-5

Lawton, Simon, 'Don't Focus on the Waves', Instagram post (22 August 2024) ☑ https://www.instagram.com/simonlawton/ (accessed 23 Aug 2024).

'Mental Health', *World Health Organization* (19 December 2019), https://www.who.int/health-topics/mental-health#tab=tab_1 (accessed 26 Mar 2025).

☑ tinyurl.com/7283-0423-9-6

Meyerowitz, Anya, '10 Things that People who Love Themselves Do', *Red* (25 November 2019), https://www.redonline.co.uk/wellbeing/a531926/self-love-habits/ (accessed 26 Mar 2025).

☑ tinyurl.com/7283-0423-9-7

Miller, Trevor, 'Understanding Desert Monasticism', [retreat talk transcript], *Northumbria Community* (17 June 2013), https://www.northumbriacommunity.org/articles/understanding-desert-monasticism/ (accessed 26 Mar 2025).

☑ tinyurl.com/ 7283-0423-9-8

O'Donohue, John, speaking to Krista Tippet on a podcast, 'The Inner Landscape of Beauty' [transcript] (28 February 2008), https://onbeing.org/programs/john-odonohue-the-inner-landscape-of-beauty/2008 (accessed 9 Jan 2025).

☑ tinyurl.com/7283-0423-9-9

Rohr, Richard, 'Purity of Heart' *Center for Action and Contemplation* (28 April 2024), https://cac.org/daily-meditations/purity-of-heart-single-mindedness/ (accessed 26 Mar 2025).

☑ tinyurl.com/7283-0423-9-10

'Saints: Saint John Berchmans', *Catholic Tradition* (undated), https://www.catholictradition.org/Mary/berchmans.htm (accessed 9 January 2025).

☑ tinyurl.com/7283-0423-9-11

Smith, Matthew, 'Three Quarters of Brits Get Less than Eight Hours Sleep', *YouGovUK* (17 January 2020), https://yougov.co.uk/health/articles/27245-three-quarters-brits-get-less-eight-hours-sleep (accessed 26 Mar 2025).

☑ tinyurl.com/7283-0423-9-12

Stolper, Jamie, 'Love Your Neighbor As Thyself ואהבת לרעך כמוך Leviticus 19:18' *Sefaria* (6 December 2020), https://www.sefaria.org/sheets/283565.1?lang=bi (accessed 26 Mar 2025).

☑ tinyurl.com/7283-0423-9-13

Valters Paintner, Christine, 'The Desert Mothers and Fathers Showed all Life is Sacred', *U.S. Catholic* (31 January 2020), https://uscatholic.org/articles/202001/discover-the-sacredness-of-life-with-the-desert-mothers-and-fathers/ (accessed 13 March 2025).

⬚ tinyurl.com/7283-0423-9-14

# SLG PRESS PUBLICATIONS

| | | |
|---|---|---|
| FP1 | *Prayer and the Life of Reconciliation* | Gilbert Shaw (1969) |
| FP2 | *Aloneness not Loneliness* | Mother Mary Clare SLG (1969) |
| FP4 | *Intercession* | Mother Mary Clare SLG (1969) |
| FP8 | *Prayer: Extracts from the Teaching of Father Gilbert Shaw* | Gilbert Shaw (1973) |
| FP12 | *Learning to Pray* | Mother Mary Clare SLG (1970, rev. 3/2025) |
| FP15 | *Death, the Gateway to Life* | Gilbert Shaw (1971, 3/2024) |
| FP16 | *The Victory of the Cross* | Dumitru Stăniloae (1970, 3/2023) |
| FP26 | *The Message of Saint Seraphim* | Irina Gorainov (1974) |
| FP28 | *Julian of Norwich: Four Studies to Commemorate the Sixth Centenary of the Revelations of Divine Love* | Sister Benedicta Ward SLG, Sister Eileen Mary SLG, Sister Mary Paul SLG, A. M. Allchin (1973, 3/2022) |
| FP43 | *The Power of the Name: The Jesus Prayer in Orthodox Spirituality* | Kallistos Ware (1974) |
| FP46 | *Prayer and Contemplation* and *Distractions are for Healing* | Robert Llewelyn (1975, rev. 4/2025) |
| FP48 | *The Wisdom of the Desert Fathers* | trans. Sister Benedicta Ward SLG (1975) |
| FP50 | *Letters of Saint Antony the Great* | trans. Derwas Chitty (1975, 2/2021) |
| FP54 | *From Loneliness to Solitude* | Roland Walls (1976) |
| FP55 | *Theology and Spirituality* | Andrew Louth (1976, rev. 1978, 3/2024) |
| FP61 | *Kabir: The Way of Love and Paradox* | Sister Rosemary SLG (1977) |
| FP62 | *Anselm of Canterbury: A Monastic Scholar* | Sister Benedicta Ward SLG (1973, 2/2024) |
| FP67 | *Mary and the Mystery of the Incarnation: An Essay on the Mother of God in the Theology of Karl Barth* | Andrew Louth (1977, 2/2024) |
| FP68 | *Trinity and Incarnation in Anglican Tradition* | A. M. Allchin (1977, rev. 2/2025) |
| FP70 | *Facing Depression* | Gonville ffrench-Beytagh (1978, 2/2020) |
| FP71 | *The Single Person* | Philip Welsh (1979) |
| FP72 | *The Letters of Ammonas, Successor of St Antony* | trans. Derwas Chitty, introd. Sebastian Brock (1979, 2/2023) |
| FP74 | *George Herbert, Priest and Poet* | Kenneth Mason (1980) |
| FP75 | *A Study of Wisdom: Three Tracts by the Author of* The Cloud of Unknowing | trans. Clifton Wolters (1980) |
| FP81 | *The Psalms: Prayer Book of the Bible* | Dietrich Bonhoeffer, trans. Sister Isabel SLG (1982, rev. 3/2025) |
| FP82 | *Prayer & Holiness: The Icon of Man Renewed in God* | Dumitru Stăniloae (1982, rev. 2/2023) |
| FP85 | *Walter Hilton: Eight Chapters on Perfection & Angels' Song* | trans. Rosemary Dorward (1983, rev. 3/2024) |
| FP88 | *Creative Suffering* | Iulia de Beausobre (1989) |
| FP90 | *Bringing Forth Christ: Five Feasts of the Child Jesus by St Bonaventure* | trans. Eric Doyle OFM (1984, 3/2024) |
| FP92 | *Gentleness in John of the Cross* | Thomas Kane (1985, rev. 2/2025) |
| FP94 | *Saint Gregory Nazianzen: Selected Poems* | trans. John McGuckin (1986, 2/2024) |
| FP95 | *The World of the Desert Fathers: Stories and Sayings from the Anonymous Series of the Apophthegmata Patrum* | trans. Columba Stewart OSB (1986, 2/2020) |
| FP104 | *Growing Old with God* | Timothy N. Rudd (1988, 2/2020) |
| FP106 | *Julian Reconsidered* | Kenneth Leech, Sister Benedicta Ward SLG (1988, rev. 2/2024) |
| FP108 | *The Unicorn: Meditations on the Love of God* | Harry Galbraith Miller (1989) |

| | | |
|---|---|---|
| FP109 | *The Creativity of Diminishment* | Sister Anke (1990) |
| FP110 | *Called to be Priests* | Hugh Wybrew (1989, updated 2/2024) |
| FP111 | *A Kind of Watershed: An Anglican Lay View of Sacramental Confession* | |
| | | Christine North (1990, updated 2/2022) |
| FP116 | *Jesus, the Living Lord* | Bishop Michael Ramsey (1992) |
| FP120 | *The Monastic Letters of Saint Athanasius the Great* | |
| | | trans. and introd. Leslie Barnard (1994, 2/2023) |
| FP122 | *The Hidden Joy* | Sister Jane SLG, ed. Dorothy Sutherland (1994) |
| FP124 | *Prayer of the Heart: An Approach to Silent Prayer and Prayer in the Night* | |
| | | Alexander Ryrie (1995, 3/2020) |
| FP126 | *Evelyn Underhill, Anglican Mystic: Two Centenary Essays* | |
| | | A. M. Allchin, Bishop Michael Ramsey (1977, rev. 4/2025) |
| FP127 | *Apostolate and the Mirrors of Paradox* | |
| | | Sydney Evans, ed. Andrew Linzey & Brian Horne (1996) |
| FP128 | *The Wisdom of Saint Isaac the Syrian* | Sebastian Brock (1997) |
| FP129 | *Saint Thérèse of Lisieux: Her Relevance for Today* | Sister Eileen Mary SLG (1997) |
| FP130 | *Expectations: Five Addresses for Those Beginning Ministry* | Sister Edmée SLG (1997, 2/2024) |
| FP131 | *Scenes from Animal Life: Fables for the Enneagram Types* | |
| | | Waltraud Kirschke, trans. Sister Isabel SLG (1998) |
| FP132 | *Praying the Word of God: The Use of Lectio Divina* | Charles Dumont OCSO (1999) |
| FP133 | *Love Unknown: Meditations on the Death and Resurrection of Jesus* | |
| | | John Barton (1999, 2/2024) |
| FP134 | *The Hidden Way of Love: Jean-Pierre de Caussade's Spirituality of Abandonment* | |
| | | Barry Conaway (1999, rev. 2/2025) |
| FP135 | *Shepherd and Servant: The Spiritual Theology of Saint Dunstan* | Douglas Dales (2000) |
| FP137 | *Pilgrimage of the Heart* | Sister Benedicta Ward SLG (2001) |
| FP138 | *Mixed Life* | Walter Hilton, trans. Rosemary Dorward (2001, enlarged rev. 3/2024) |
| FP139 | *In the Footsteps of the Lord: The Teaching of Abba Isaiah of Scetis* | |
| | | John Chryssavgis, Luke Penkett (2001, 2/2023) |
| FP140 | *A Great Joy: Reflections on the Meaning of Christmas* | Kenneth Mason (2001) |
| FP141 | *Bede and the Psalter* | Sister Benedicta Ward SLG (2002, 2/2024) |
| FP142 | *Abhishiktananda: A Memoir of Dom Henri Le Saux* | Murray Rogers, David Barton (2003) |
| FP143 | *Friendship in God: The Encounter of Evelyn Underhill & Sorella Maria of Campello* | |
| | | A. M. Allchin (2003, rev. 2/2025) |
| FP144 | *Christian Imagination in Poetry and Polity: Some Anglican Voices from Temple to Herbert* | |
| | | Bishop Rowan Williams (2004) |
| FP145 | *The Reflections of Abba Zosimas: Monk of the Palestinian Desert* | |
| | | trans. and introd. John Chryssavgis (2005, 3/2022) |
| FP146 | *The Gift of Theology: The Trinitarian Vision of Ann Griffiths and Elizabeth of Dijon* | |
| | | A. M. Allchin (2005) |
| FP147 | *Sacrifice and Spirit* | Bishop Michael Ramsey (2005) |
| FP148 | *Saint John Cassian on Prayer* | trans. A. M. Casiday (2006, 2/2024) |
| FP149 | *Hymns of Saint Ephrem the Syrian* | trans. Mary Hansbury (2006, 2/2024) |
| FP150 | *Suffering: Why All this Suffering? What Do I Do about It?* | |
| | | Reinhard Körner OCD, trans. Sister Avis Mary SLG (2006) |
| FP151 | *A True Easter: The Synod of Whitby 664 AD* | Sister Benedicta Ward SLG (2007, 2/2023) |
| FP152 | *Prayer as Self-Offering* | Alexander Ryrie (2007) |
| FP153 | *From Perfection to the Elixir: How George Herbert Fashioned a Famous Poem* | |
| | | Benedick de la Mare (2008, 2/2024) |
| FP154 | *The Jesus Prayer: Gospel Soundings* | Sister Pauline Margaret CHN (2008) |

| | | |
|---|---|---|
| FP155 | *Loving God Whatever: Through the Year with Sister Jane* | Sister Jane SLG (2006) |
| FP156 | *Prayer and Meditation for a Sleepless Night* | |
| | | SISTERS OF THE LOVE OF GOD (1993, 3/2024) |
| FP157 | *Being There: Caring for the Bereaved* | John Porter (2009) |
| FP158 | *Learn to Be at Peace: The Practice of Stillness* | Andrew Norman (2010) |
| FP159 | *From Holy Week to Easter* | George Pattison (2010) |
| FP160 | *Strength in Weakness: The Scandal of the Cross* | John W. Rogerson (2010) |
| FP161 | *Augustine Baker: Frontiers of the Spirit* | Victor de Waal (2010, rev. 2/2025) |
| FP162 | *Out of the Depths* | |
| | | Gonville ffrench-Beytagh; epilogue Wendy Robinson (1990, 2/2010) |
| FP163 | *God and Darkness: A Carmelite Perspective* | |
| | | Gemma Hinricher OCD, trans. Sister Avis Mary SLG (2010) |
| FP164 | *The Gift of Joy* | Curtis Almquist SSJE (2011) |
| FP165 | *'I Have Called You Friends': Suggestions for the Spiritual Life Based on the Farewell Discourses of Jesus* | Reinhard Körner OCD (2012) |
| FP166 | *Leisure* | Mother Mary Clare SLG (2012) |
| FP167 | *Carmelite Ascent: An Introduction to Saint Teresa and Saint John of the Cross* | |
| | | Mother Mary Clare SLG (1973, rev. 2/2012) |
| FP168 | *Ann Griffiths and Her Writings* | Llewellyn Cumings (2012) |
| FP169 | *The Our Father* | Sister Benedicta Ward SLG (2012) |
| FP171 | *The Spiritual Wisdom of the Syriac Book of Steps* | Robert A. Kitchen (2013) |
| FP172 | *The Prayer of Silence* | Alexander Ryrie (2012) |
| FP173 | *On Tour in Byzantium: Excerpts from The Spiritual Meadow of John Moschus* | |
| | | Ralph Martin SSM (2013) |
| FP174 | *Monastic Life* | Bonnie Thurston (2016) |
| FP175 | *Shall All Be Well? Reflections for Holy Week* | Graham Ward (2015) |
| FP176 | *Solitude and Communion: Papers on the Hermit Life* | ed. A. M. Allchin (2015) |
| FP177 | *The Prayers of Jacob of Serugh* | ed. Mary Hansbury (2015) |
| FP178 | *The Monastic Hours of Prayer* | Sister Benedicta Ward SLG (2016) |
| FP179 | *The Desert of the Heart: Daily Readings with the Desert Fathers* | |
| | | trans. Sister Benedicta Ward SLG (2016) |
| FP180 | *In Company with Christ: Lent, Palm Sunday, Good Friday & Easter to Pentecost* | |
| | | Sister Benedicta Ward SLG (2016) |
| FP181 | *Lazarus: Come Out! Reflections on John 11* | Bonnie Thurston (2017) |
| FP182 | *Unknowing & Astonishment: Meditations on Faith for the Long Haul* | |
| | | Christopher Scott (2018) |
| FP183 | *Pondering, Praying, Preaching: Romans 8* | Bonnie Thurston (2019, 2/2021) |
| FP184 | *Shem`on the Graceful: Discourse on the Solitary Life* | |
| | | trans. and introd. Mary Hansbury (2020) |
| FP185 | *God Under My Roof: Celtic Songs and Blessings* | Esther de Waal (2020) |
| FP186 | *Journeying with the Jesus Prayer* | James F. Wellington (2020) |
| FP187 | *Poet of the Word: Re-reading Scripture with Ephraem the Syrian* | Aelred Partridge OC (2020) |
| FP188 | *Identity and Ritual* | Alan Griffiths (2021) |
| FP189 | *River of the Spirit: The Spirituality of Simon Barrington-Ward* | Andy Lord (2021) |
| FP190 | *Prayer and the Struggle against Evil* | John Barton, Daniel Lloyd, |
| | | James Ramsay, Alexander Ryrie (2021) |
| FP191 | *Dante's Spiritual Journey: A Reading of the Divine Comedy* | Tony Dickinson (2021) |
| FP192 | *Jesus the Undistorted Image of God* | John Townroe (2022) |
| FP193 | *Our Deepest Desire: Prayer, Fasting & Almsgiving in the Writings of Saint Augustine of Hippo* | Sister Susan SLG (2022) |

| | | |
|---|---|---|
| FP194 | Lent with George Herbert | Tony Dickinson (2022) |
| FP195 | Four Ways to the Cross | Tony Dickinson (2022) |
| FP196 | Anselm of Canterbury, Teacher of Prayer | Sister Benedicta Ward SLG (2022) |
| FP197 | With One Heart and Mind: Prayers out of Stillness | Anthony Kemp (2023) |
| FP198 | Sayings of the Urban Fathers & Mothers | James Ashdown (2023) |
| FP199 | Doors | Sister Raphael SLG (2023) |
| FP200 | Monastic Vocation    SISTERS OF THE LOVE OF GOD, | Bishop Rowan Williams (2021) |
| FP201 | An Ecology of the Heart: Faith Through the Climate Crisis | Duncan Forbes (2023) |
| FP202 | 'In the image of the Image': Gregory of Nyssa's Opposition to Slavery | Adam Couchman (2023) |
| FP203 | Gregory of Nyssa and the Sins of Asia Minor | Jonathan Farrugia (2023) |
| FP204 | Discovery | Arthur Bell (2023) |
| FP205 | Living Healing: The Spirituality of Leanne Payne | Andy Lord (2023) |
| FP206 | Still Listening: Sowing the Seeds of the Jesus Prayer | Bruce Batstone CJN (2023) |
| FP207 | Julian of Norwich: Four Essays to Commemorate 650 Years of the Revelations of Divine Love    Bishop Graham Usher, Father Colin CSWG, Sister Elizabeth Ruth Obbard OC, Mother Hilary Crupi OJN (2023) | |
| FP208 | TIME | Dumitru Stăniloae, Kallistos Ware (2023) |
| FP209 | Pearls of Life: A Lifebelt for the Spirit | Tony Dickinson (2024) |
| FP210 | The Way and the Truth and the Life: An Exploration by a Follower of the Way | James Ramsay (2024) |
| FP211 | Cosmos, Crisis & Christ: Essays of Wendy Robinson | Wendy Robinson (2024) |
| FP212 | Towards a Theology of Psychotherapy: The Spirituality of Wendy Robinson | Andrew Louth (2024) |
| FP213 | Immersed in God and the World: Living Priestly Ministry | Andy Lord (2024) |
| FP214 | The Road to Emmaus: A Sculptor's Journey through Time | Rodney Munday (2024) |
| FP215 | Prayer Too Deep for Words | Sister Edmée SLG (2024) |
| FP216 | The Prayers of St Isaac of Nineveh | Sebastian Brock (2024) |
| FP217 | Two Medieval English Saints: Cuthbert and Alban | Sister Benedicta Ward SLG (2024) |
| FP218 | Encountering the Depths | Mother Mary Clare SLG (1981, rev. 3/2024) |
| FP219 | Conflict and Concord    Sister Susan SLG, Bishop Humphrey Southern, Bronwen Neil, Sister Rosemary SLG, Sister Clare-Louise SLG (2024) | |
| FP220 | Divine Love in the Song of Songs | Sister Edmée SLG (2024) |
| FP221 | Zeal for the Faith: An Introduction to Christian-Muslim Dialogue | Tony Dickinson (2024) |
| FP222 | Bernard & Abelard | Sister Edmée SLG (2024) |
| FP223 | Eliot's Transitions: T. S. Eliot's Search for Identity and the Society of the Sacred Mission at Kelham Hall | Vincent Strudwick (2024) |
| FP224 | Landscape, Soul and Spirit: Ecology, Prayer and Robert Macfarlane | Andy Lord (2025) |
| FP225 | Our Home is in God | John Townroe (2025) |
| FP226 | Signs of the Times: A Brief Survey of the Bible's Apocalyptic Writings | Tony Dickinson (2025) |
| FP227 | And We Shall be Changed: Christian Reflections on Death and Dying | James Ramsay (2025) |
| FP228 | Journeys into the Bible | Sister Edmée SLG (2025) |
| FP229 | Directions | Sister Edmée SLG (2025) |
| FP230 | Loving Yourself | Richard Frost (2025) |
| FP231 | Angels | Sister Raphael SLG (2025) |

www.slgpress.co.uk

## Contemplative Poetry Series

| | | |
|---|---|---|
| CP1 | *Amado Nervo: Poems of Faith and Doubt* | trans. John Gallas (2021) |
| CP2 | *Anglo-Saxon Poets: The High Roof of Heaven* | trans. John Gallas (2021) |
| CP3 | *Middle English Poets: Where Grace Grows Ever Green* | ed. John Gallas (2021) |
| CP4 | *The Voice inside Our Home: Selected Poems* | Edward Clarke (2022) |
| CP5 | *Women & God: Drops in the Sea of Time* | trans. and ed. John Gallas (2022) |
| CP6 | *Gabrielle de Coignard & Vittoria Colonna: Fly Not Too High* | trans. John Gallas (2022) |
| CP7 | *Chancing on Sanctity: Selected Poems* | James Ramsay (2022) |
| CP8 | *Gabriela Mistral: This Far Place* | trans. John Gallas (2023) |
| CP9 | *Henry Vaughan & George Herbert: Divine Themes and Celestial Praise* | ed. Edward Clarke (2023) |
| CP10 | *Love Will Come with Fire: Anthology* | Sisters of the Love of God (2023) |
| CP11 | *Touchpapers: Anthology* | coll. and trans. John Gallas (2023) |
| CP12 | *Seasons of my Soul: Selected Poems* | Clare McKerron (2023) |
| CP13 | *Reinhard Sorge: Take Flight to God* | trans. John Gallas (2024) |
| CP14 | *Embertide: Encountering Saint Frideswide* | Romola Parish (2024) |
| CP15 | *Thomas Campion: Made All of Light* | ed. and introd. Julia Craig-McFeely (2024) |
| CP16 | *When God Hides: Selected Poems* | Joseph Evans (2025) |

## Vestry Guides

| | | |
|---|---|---|
| VG1 | *The Visiting Minister: How to Welcome Visiting Clergy to Your Church* | Paul Monk (2021) |
| VG2 | *Help! No Minister! or Please Take the Service* | Paul Monk (2022) |
| VG3 | *The Liturgy of the Eucharist: An Introductory Guide* | Paul Monk (2024) |

## www.slgpress.co.uk

---

The Sisters of the Love of God is an Anglican community of women religious living a contemplative monastic life.

To learn more about the Community and the Convent of the Incarnation at Fairacres, Oxford, see our website www.slg.org.uk.

As well as supporting those seeking to follow a vocation to the monastic life, the Community has a number of forms of association for those who feel drawn to share in the Sisters' life of prayer: Fellowship of the Love of God, Companions, Priests Associate or Oblate Sisters.

For more information email sisters@slg.org.uk or write to The Reverend Mother, Convent of the Incarnation, Parker Street, Oxford, OX4 1TB, UK.